THE
OUTRAGEOUS
LIMERICK BOOK

Over 250 Rhymes
Against Nature

by

A. Reimer

Tripro
BOOKS

Printed in the United States of America
ISBN 0-943392-63-2

First Edition: June 1984

1 2 3 4 5 6 7 8 9 10

Introduction

I am frequently called upon by listeners both shocked and amused to enlighten them about the origin of the art form that slithers across the following pages. For some time I was content to simply say, "I dunno," and people seemed relieved that this dead end gave them the opportunity to change the topic to something classier, like dead baby jokes. One day, however, I happened to stumble on an entry concerning this peculiar form of verse in the encyclopedia (I'd been looking to brush up on "Liquefaction" for party chitchat), and learned a few interesting facts.

Limericks originated in—go ahead, say "County Cork"—where else but County Limerick. (That's in Ireland, for all of you who got Ds in Geography, and Ireland is in Europe, for all of you who got Fs.) Way back then Limerick wasn't yet the jet-set mecca we consider it now. People would gather at the village pub to pump travelers for news of the outside world, using a ritual sort of song in which each verse ended, "Ah, but have you been to Limerick?" Gradually (a useful Gaelic word which translates into English as "Don't ask me, I don't know the details"), the songs were standardized into five lines with a rhyme scheme of *aabba,* and the interrogative aspect of the poems was dropped. (Probably because the villagers got tired of hearing the question that ended each stanza answered "No" every time.)

The encyclopedia didn't specify when all this happened, but we can probably surmise that it was not B.C. but more likely recent A.D., since nowhere in the Bible is Jesus quoted saying things like "Dear Peter, you've been like a brother. . . .And Johnny, take care of my mother."

Some famous limericists include Edward Lear and Ogden Nash, but these guys copped out in my opinion by frequently beginning and ending their limericks with the same line, e.g., "There once was a man from Nantucket. . . .That crazy old man from Nantucket." I mean, how hard can it be to come up with an extra seven or eight syllables?

Which brings us—don't worry, it's nearly over—to how and why one writes limericks. Myself, I prefer nonvulgar limericks (yes, I *am* weird), having been first inspired by the brilliant nonsensical ones by Edward Gorey. I freely admit, however, that the limerick lends itself more readily to scuz and slime.

4

When transporting manuscript to my publishers I wear a disguise. I leave all incriminating I.D. at home, in case I'm hit by a bus, but conspicuously pin a note to my jacket explaining that I wrote the stuff on the scattered papers around my body under duress, which should be good for *some* sympathetic treatment from the emergency room staff.

As to why I write limericks, I plead genetics. I'd been writing them to my own bewilderment for some time before it dawned on me that my ancestors spent *their* evenings in pubs in County Limerick, scaring the tourists away.

There's no escaping the awful truth, then—limericks are in my blood.

Outrageous

I used to ball chicks by the score
But just like Poe said, "Nevermore!"
My favorite lay, Dinah,
Screamed, "Not *my* vagina!"
And freaked over one little sore.

━━■━━

I'm sorry I caused such a row
But that's all behind us for now
There's something between us
—I think it's your penis—
We have to get straight—HOLY COW!

━━■━━

My mom's voice ascended in pitch
And the dread secret caused her to twitch
"I'm not an Alsatian
I'm just a Dalmatian
You're *really* a son of a bitch!"

Limericks

We felt very sorry for Keith
Who bade *bon voyage* to his sheath
Things weren't as he'd dreamed
He learned when he screamed
"Good God, Maryanne—it's got teeth!"

Our orgy—well, none could prevent it
Though you were left out, don't resent it
But hot damn! What fucking
And Jesus, the sucking!
When we screamed, "Here we come!", man, we *meant* it.

My girlfriend was easy to teach
I learned late one night at the beach
I said, "Babe, let's fuck
But remember, now, *suck*
'Cause blow's just a figure of speech."

Outrageous

Pierre was so deeply engrossed
He lingered much longer than most
He stayed on to savor
The prostitute's flavor
Which tasted like pussy on toast.

━━■━━

"I blew my exam," blubbered Coral
But "Never give up" is our moral
Though she fucked up the written
The student sex kitten
Next day simply sailed through the oral.

━━■━━

I wish now I'd just sent a wreath
Instead, stupid me did bequeath
An heirloom too reckless
—A double-strand necklace
I'd made from our dead children's teeth.

Limericks

The recipe said to begin
With carrion flesh soaked in gin
Then season with scabies
And hair from dead babies
Voilà! Sit right down and dig in!

———■———

I made Porky Pig into juice
And steak from Bullwinkle the Moose
The croquettes, by the way,
And the liver paté
I made out of dear Mother Goose.

———■———

There's something I want to make clear
You do have a glorious rear
But please don't get pushy
I'll get to your tushy
As soon as I'm done with your ear.

Outrageous

Two butch guys were working up heat
When one said, "You call this stuff sweet?
You said, 'Suck my custard'
It tastes more like mustard
So please keep it off of my meat."

═ ■ ═

Too frightened to speak off the cuff
I lied and admired her stuff:
'What a pretty fur hat!
By the way, where's your cat?
You don't say! By the way, love the muff!"

═ ■ ═

The butcher complained to his daughter
"A cow is so boring to slaughter
But not this salami
It used to be Mommy
She ran seven blocks 'til I caught her."

Limericks

Forgive me for coming on strong
I guess that I just might be wrong
But really now, Stanley
Do you think it's manly
To sit on my dildo this long?

=—■—=

An M on each cheek painted Tom
While I feared our sex was a bomb
I said, "Stop your stalling
It's time we were balling
Bend over and show me your MOM."

=—■—=

A silver tycoon in Tobruk
Quite relished the pleasure he took
In fucking his chauffeur
(A profligate loafer)
Who afterwards sucked off the cook.

Outrageous

The witch doctor said, "I'm the best
Obey me and soon you'll be blessed
Two shots of fresh guano
Straight up with Chinzanno
Will really put hair on your chest."

═ ■ ═

The widow at first was nonplussed
But gamely resolved to adjust
She reached in the casket
And patted his basket
And sighed, "Oh well, lust unto dust."

═ ■ ═

Though Martians all claim they're the best
I fear that I'm not too impressed
On Neptune the he-men
Shoot 90-proof semen
That really puts hair on your chest.

Limericks

I have no regrets, dear, do you?
Who cares if we broke a taboo
I don't think it's spooky
It's simply—well, kooky
But though you're a corpse, I love you.

—■—

The timid groom swallowed his pride
And said, "Parson, I need a guide"
Soon after the pastor
Moaned, "Good, but go faster
And do it like this with your bride."

—■—

The peg-leg corsair, Captain Hood
Would screw every hostage he could
Though captives would beg
They soon learned his leg
Was not *all* he had made of wood.

Outrageous

When Santa got eager to ball
He entered his first reindeer's stall
His coal eyes were gleaming
And all heard him screaming
"Cum, Dasher! Cum, Prancer! Cum *ALL!*"

— ■ —

Young Megan, a comely young Scotch
Is so entertaining to watch
Her gifted vagina
Can squawk like a minah
Moreover, she smiles with her crotch.

— ■ —

Quite dangerous proved young Yvonne
We learned as we balled on the lawn
Her overstretched anus
Could more than contain us
Why, Bobby slipped in and was gone!

Limericks

The cannibals answered our greeting
And told us they'd catered our meeting
Said one, "We're bereft
Since the witch doctor left
But damn! Don't his balls make good eating?"

———■———

My friend cried, "You call that film nice?
That couple was covered with lice
And their scene on the desk
Was so lewd and grotesque
I barely could sit through it twice."

———■———

The skydiving nudist who vowed
A Grand Canyon bullseye was proud
When over the chasm
He had an orgasm
That ruined nine hats in the crowd.

Outrageous

I balled with a hot electrician
Who really knew every position
But he was a bummer
Compared to the plumber
Whose wrench put my pipes in condition.

— ■ —

A monster, half-dolphin, half-minah
Was found beached in North Carolina
They said that the creature
Could boast no best feature
—Except for its four-foot vagina.

— ■ —

To virtue let's bid fond farewell
My book will corrupt you pell-mell
By noon each beginner
Has waxed such a sinner
By midnight he's roasting in hell!

Limericks

My virgin bride dealt me a shock
And I, thunderstruck, had to gawk
I cried, "Holy shit!"
When I saw that her clit
Was three times as big as my cock.

=—■—=

Displaying the knife, still in shock
I told how the menacing jock
Said, "You won't need those"
(Which referred to my clothes)
And I said the same re his cock.

=—■—=

Insatiably horny Monique
Picked up quite a muscular Greek
And between massive thighs
She found such a surprise
That she couldn't walk for a week.

Outrageous

The ad was abundant with flesh
As pussy encased in black mesh
Said, 'Treat your clitoris
And douche with Laboris
And take home a crotch kissing fresh!"

— ■ —

The agency answered the dare
And hired a blonde to declare
"Nocturnal Emissions
Deep cleans and conditions
And puts sparkle back in your hair."

— ■ —

Babette had a real eager beaver
And, baring it, dared me to leave her
I said, "As you please
First stop licking your knees!"
Once she did, I was glad to relieve her.

Limericks

Ramon spent a week on my farm
Where his Latin eyes worked like a charm
What he brought to our tryst
Was as thick as his wrist
And to boot twice as long as his arm.

Consider that Netherlands tyke
Who freely abandoned his bike
Then, truly unselfish,
Swore he could smell shellfish
But still stuck his thumb in the dyke.

My nightmares each night get much worse
As I scream at a whole universe
Of afterbirthquakes
And fresh mother's-milkshakes
And things I'd call yet more perverse.

Outrageous

Although I'll admit I'm still young
You wouldn't believe how I'm hung
And you'll just flip your wig
Because though it's big
It's small by far than my tongue.

— ∎ —

I don't give a damn what you've read
Let's call the mortician instead
Now, please, your suggestion
Is out of the question
A blow job's no good to the dead.

— ∎ —

My girlfriend, Elise, in mid-screw
Dealt me such a shock I withdrew:
"Don't mean to be funny
But is it true, honey
That if I have the clap, so do you?"

Limericks

The farmer who lived in the dell
Showed off what he had by the well
A tisket, a tasket
The size of his basket
Made Mary contrary as hell.

———■———

A shortage of men is not new
But sex now's so long overdue
That last night in slumber
I dreamt a cucumber
Was crooning "It Had To Be You."

———■———

The truth is that as I undressed
I felt both unsure and distressed
But he was so gentle
I waxed sentimental
And now I know Father knows best.

Outrageous

Tonight I had Linda and Jill
And then Mary, Susie, and Lil
I've nicknamed my nieces
"The Five Easy Pieces"
Though nephews are easier still.

———■———

The Tin Man pursued his release
With Munchkins who loved to caprice
The sweat from these binges
Fast rusted his hinges
Till Dorothy whipped out the grease.

———■———

The captain, in mid-dress review
Decided he just had to screw
He fucked the armed forces
(To boot, all their horses)
And most of the spectators, too.

Limericks

Don't worry, my li'l chickadee
It's simple as ol' A-B-C:
Midway through my pushup
You just lift your tush up
And then leave the details to me.

=—■—=

The hotshot was quite mortified
When two girls he'd pinched up and cried
"We girls don't make passes
At men with fat asses
So, Blubberbutt, just step aside!"

=—■—=

French whores, when his cock was revealed
Turned pale but consented to yield
One thought, "It's enormous!
It's bound to deform us
Good thing we've got Bleu Cross/Bleu Shield!"

Outrageous

The cuckold, too good for this life
Was slow on the draw with his knife
He caught two homewreckers
And cut off their peckers
But not 'til they'd done with his wife.

— ∎ —

Sinderella, the X-rated flick
Was lurid, perverted, and sick
That scene on the wharf!
(Seven girls and one dwarf)
How *did* they all fit on his dick?

— ∎ —

The X-rated actress, Big Lil
Had pussy that nothing could fill
In North Carolina
They dubbed her vagina
"The Pussy That Ate Chapel Hill."

Limericks

A flasher, profaning in Rome
Was told 'neath the Vatican's dome
"You're really too paunchy
For language so raunchy
So zip up your fly and go home!"

— ∎ —

My taste buds were in for a treat
When I set the table to eat
A stew of soiled panties
From two favorite aunties
Whose tampons made dinner complete.

— ∎ —

The animal lover I'm dating
Required this mild castigating:
"I'm glad you're so smitten
But put down that kitten
'Cause this pussy's tired of waiting."

Outrageous

A star on the soaps yesterday
Was quite overwhelmed by dismay
A love scene had started
When he up and farted
And blew his poor co-star away.

— ■ —

Elaine said, "I've nothing to hide
In fact, my large twat is my pride
So large was the hole
When I said, "Let's go bowl"
She set up the tenpins inside.

— ■ —

Though nothing was quite like a dame
The zookeeper went for wild game
He balled with two leopards
Because German Shepherds
He found were all right but too tame.

Limericks

I'm rarin' to go until dawn
And can't wait to just get it on
I love when you spank me
And J. Arthur Rank me
But, Grandpa, what *have* you got on?

———■———

The teacher was licking her lips
And straddled a sophomore's hips
Thank goodness her pupils
Had not heard of scruples
Or they'd say, "Goodbye, Mrs. Chips."

———■———

A bonny young blonde shepherdess
Stood by while her friend did undress
When he lifted his kilt
She could see that his hilt
Looked like someone she knew from Loch Ness.

Outrageous

A priest, at his bishops' discretion,
Was happy to make the concession
Of lifting his cassock
And, straddling the hassock,
Began to unfold his confession.

—■—

Oppressed by a vague sense of dread
I stood at the foot of their bed
My folks were reluctant
To tell me what "fuck" meant
But offered to show me instead.

—■—

Exotic erotica's fine
As long as you keep it in line
But poor cousin Herman
Was queer for a merman
And drowned as they did 69.

Limericks

I hope it will not make you mad
Because all in all you're not bad
But though it was heaven
The sad truth is, Kevin
That no one gives head like your dad.

— ■ —

My girlfriend last night was so hot
That, really, believe it or not
Steam poured our her ear
While flames shot from her rear
And tendrils of smoke from her twat.

— ■ —

My roommate said, "Gee, home so soon?"
I answered, "God damn that Calhoun!
I'm really disgusted
His cock was encrusted
With sores each as big as the moon."

Outrageous

From pregnancy you can escape
But needn't resort to "the scrape"
These lively contortions
Cost less than abortions
And, furthermore, keep you in shape.

═─■─═

His cock was more fit for a sparrow
To boot, his urethra was narrow
Then drugs intravenous
Were fed to his penis
And—PRESTO!—it willed a wheelbarrow.

═─■─═

A cowboy was sitting astraddle
And rubbing his buns on his saddle
He told his friend Zeke
"Why, it's been a whole week
Since I've had a taste of the paddle."

Limericks

The cathouse was really a treasure
And Madam said, "Sir, for your pleasure
Once done with the camel
You'll find that the ram'll
Be able to take your full measure."

— ∎ —

His cousin said, "Honestly, Clive
I'm just overwhelmed by your drive
We'll got to the nooky
But first have a cookie
My gosh but you're horny for five."

— ∎ —

An S & M couple were balling
When Mister S said, "Cut the stalling!"
Miss M said, "Please, Master
I wish you'd go faster
The roof beam's on fire—and it's falling!"

Outrageous

She turned for advice to a friend
Who asked, "Just how much can you spend?
'Cause measure for measure
You'll get twice the pleasure
From dildos with heads on each end."

—■—

The black man said, "White folks are crass
Although just to watch they're a gas
I once saw a honky
Go down on a donkey
And call it a good piece of ass."

—■—

We went out to wrestle in mud
But my lust was nipped in the bud
I said, "Let's start kissing"
She thought I said "pissing"
And I nearly drowned in the flood.

Limericks

My brother, believe it or not
Burst in just when things had grown hot
He said, "Listen, Mister
Stop fucking my sister!
It's high time she gave me a shot."

———■———

My father, who knew no taboo
Confessed what I knew to be true:
"You know, son, your mother
Gives head like no other
—Except for your sister and you."

———■———

My first book's enjoyed quite a sale
Though it's the unlikeliest tale
It's purely escapist
And tells of a rapist
Who actually goes off to jail.

Outrageous

Our neighbor, who looks like a dream
Is dumber than dumb it would seem
So slow on the uptake
When I called her "Cupcake"
She said, "But I'm not filled with cream."

—■—

From fiery passion an ember
Has lasted long after September
Tonight I grew wistful
Recalling your fistful
And came singing "Try to Remember."

—■—

My girlfriend was fond of a stunt
In which I would drop-kick or punt
A ball down the field
And we knew when she squealed
That she's caught the damn thing with her cunt.

Limericks

Though glad for a midwife on board
Her strange bedside mien we deplored
For as we passed Dover
She blithely leaned over
And chewed through—and swallowed—the cord.

—■—

Sweet Nell cried, "Betrayal, alas!
I shan't stray again from my class
For thanks to the villain
I need penicillin
Oh, dear! What a pain in the ass!"

—■—

Last weekend I earned a black eye
For standing too close to a guy
When he said to back off
I though I heard "jack off"
With which I was quick to comply.

Outrageous

A wet tee shirt contest in Dallas
Was won and then lost by poor Alice
The judge gasped, "Her nipples!
Good golly, they're triples!
And damn if she ain't got a phallus!"

—■—

I warned you that contest was sick
But that was a hell of a trick
She proved she could handle
A five-foot long candle
When out of her nose came the wick.

—■—

I really don't like to complain
But I can't perform when in pain
So come to the stable
But show me you're able
To be both a stud and humane.

Limericks

They say that good things come in twos
And so I'll be glad to reuse
My sister's placenta
It's just the magenta
I needed to dye my new shoes.

My mother sat up in her bed
And beckoned me to her instead
She whispered, "Don't bother
To wake up your father
'Cause I'll gladly give you some head."

The minute he turned ninety-two
Old Harry succumbed to the flu
To heaven transported
He soon was rewarded
With pussy too good to be true.

Outrageous

The great burlesque legend Louise
Succumbed to a fatal disease
But still fairly often
She rose from her coffin
To bump and grind through a cryptease.

= ■ =

Relieved that I'd not gone to Hell
My dark thoughts began to dispel
But wandering in Limbo
I there met a bimbo
I'd fucked back on Earth in Carmel.

= ■ =

The camera crew got a bad fright
And shooting shut down for the night
Instead of an eagle
The zoo sent a beagle
Which didn't survive its first flight.

Limericks

Us girls think that group sex is hot
So each night at ten on the dot
We lower the lights
And lower our tights
And have us a *menáge a* twat.

═══■═══

They say you're a woman to fear
But you don't appear so from here
Who cares if you're vicious
I think you're delicious
—Though you could use mayo in here.

═══■═══

A toddler who came uninvited
To visit his parents was frighted
And neglecting to knock
He sustained quite a shock
But his folks in mid-fuck were delighted.

Outrageous

In Milan he was struck with lumbago
So, unable to go where the gay go
He hired an Italian
A swarthy young stallion
All they said was: "Oh, *grazie!*" "*Prego.*"

———■———

I fear I've some bad news about
An ailment more dreadful than gout
It's said the disease
Makes you cum when you sneeze
—God bless you! *Gesundheit!* Get out!

———■———

The Abbess was deeply offended
Monsignor had called her butt "splendid"
He said, "A bad habit
I have is to grab it
And see that it's warmly befriended."

Limericks

Right here on this overgrown mound
Is where the authorities found
The still-frozen sturgeon
Stuck up in the virgin
See? There's still a smile on the ground.

—■—

A horny gay Sergeant First Class
Was granted a full weekend pass
Then, using a stencil
He managed to pencil
The words "Enter Here" on his ass.

—■—

The hooker was greatly displeased
When Monday's first trick up and sneezed
And left her poor twat
Overflowing with snot
Which she later learned was diseased.

Outrageous

The hot ladies-only club "Mars"
Has nude men on each of the bars
The chicks love the stripper
Who's billed "The Big Dipper"
'Cause when he fucks you, you see stars.

— ■ —

That unsympathetic McGirk
Said this when his wife went beserk:
"Big deal, so you're dying!
Would you quit your crying
Or I'll be late getting to work."

— ■ —

The hillbilly whore Mary Lou
Told Parson a hot thing or two
"How I makes my living
Don't need no forgiving
'Cause dead folks need tenderness, too."

Limericks

The critic attended my play
But said in the paper next day
"The daughter's instructor
Ran downstage and fucked her!
—A scene I thought *almost* risqué."

=—■—=

The plantiff wailed, "This is God's truth!
That dentist is simply uncouth
I asked for a filling
So he started drilling
But *waaay* to the south of my tooth."

=—■—=

Take "Mother Goose" down from the shelf
And read me the one where the elf
Said, "I'm gonna stuff it
In Little Miss Muffet"
But lacked what was needed himself.

Outrageous

The Pope caught a whiff of the gas
And sighed as he thought at high mass
"It's said he who smelt it
Is he who hath dealt it
O Lord, put Thy cork up my ass."

———■———

You kids are great fun, but it's late
—Okay, but no later than eight
But now let's trade places
You sit on *our* faces
And we'll try to tell you your weight.

———■———

I only insist that you're clean
Who cares if you're not long and lean
Don't worry; my hubby
Prefers his men chubby
—Oh, didn't I mention Eugene?

Limericks

Please tell me the truth, won't you, Fred?
Aren't we older chicks good in bed?
Last night was pure heaven
Too bad you're eleven
By the time you're my age, I'll be dead.

— ■ —

His act, more than just lacking class
Was vulgar, disgusting, and crass
For he—ugh—picked his nose
Not with fingers, but toes
And smoked a cigar with his ass.

— ■ —

King Henry was quite true to form
When he, in the midst of a storm,
Sat straight up in bed
And yelled, "Off with her head!"
And came while the corpse was still warm.

Outrageous

The poor man was sick with drustration
Surviving on mere masturbation
For each time it got rigid
His wife would go frigid
And say a firm "No" to fellation.

— ∎ —

The gardener loved every rose
And struck the most pastoral pose
While watering the flowers
With warm golden showers
That poured from a curious hose.

— ∎ —

I hope you've no great expectations
Because I have grave reservations
No, I couldn't indulge
—But one glimpse of your bulge
Negates all my good aspirations.

Limericks

I moaned as she clambered on top
And prayed that we never would stop
She was just outasight
With a twat so airtight
That when I pulled out it went "Pop!"

—■—

Well, that's the last time I'll see him!
'Cause, granted, he's handsome and slim
But last night in bed
When I gave him some head
I learned why he's called "Tiny Tim."

—■—

The whore said, "Of course I look sour!
I never have time for a shower
I'm glad I'm successful
But, damn, it's so stressful
To lay fifteen men every hour."

Outrageous

"I'm somewhat embarrassed," said Keith
To Midge, who was busy beneath
"See, I'm not really gray
—That's a pubic toupée
That's left plastic curls in your teeth."

—— ■ ——

You betcha I like my men tough
And sure I dig sex when it's rough
But, shit, I'm so bruised
We are *quite* unamused
Besides, fourteen times is enough!

—— ■ ——

My teenage son wanted to rap
So I said, "Okay, son—no crap:
When making advances
You just take your chances
And pray that she ain't got the clap."

Limericks

Why, Merlin, thou old motherfucker!
Nay, marry, that's right—not a pucker!
There's no way I could
Have misunderstood
What thou couldst have meant by "seersucker."

———■———

The cult by whose laws I am bound
Performs a rite odd but profound
We eat raw intestine
And so are clandestine
For there's not enough to go 'round.

———■———

The wizard's display was so crass
No wonder the crowd cried, "Alas!"
He yelled, "Hocus-pocus!"
And that's when a crocus
Bloomed right as we watched from his ass.

Outrageous

Aunt Ida, though sweet as can be
Grossed out both my sister and me
With "Girls, don't forget
To save me your sweat
It's great as a base for iced tea."

—■—

I blushed, wanting not to deflower
This girl from the ivory tower
'Til she said, "You see
My favors aren't free
In fact, I get ninety an hour."

—■—

My "grouch" reputation aside
I'm really quite proud to confide
I love little tots
Though they give me the trots
When served up with rice on the side.

Limericks

I'm sorry I have to renege
Yes, sir, I can see that it's big
It ain't that I'm scared
I'm just unprepared
For what Madam meant by a "pig."

———■———

You've brought such a blush to my skin
I just can't extinguish my grin
A great blow job, Mother!
May I have another?
That is, when you're done with my twin?

———■———

The necrophile called to his bride
"Now, darling, please let me inside
You misunderstood
When I said how good
It feels to love someone's who's died."

Outrageous

The nuptials were held in late June
Which seemed not a moment too soon
Halfway through the wedding
The bride started shedding
Her gown for a hot honeymoon.

━■━

My folks both approved of my Mabel
Especially Dad, who said, "Abel,
This girl is some catch
I fingered her snatch
While we were all seated at table."

━■━

I plan a career in hard porn
Because I hold virtue in scorn
I'll break all the strictures
With X-rated pictures
Hot damn! I can't wait to be born!

Limericks

Though some say our love is obscene
I'll never give up my Pauline
She's cheerful and sunny
And wonderfully funny
And very mature for thirteen.

———■———

Punctilious Madam Babette
Instructed the new girl, Yvette:
"Now, always be clean
And say what you mean
—Except the words, 'Ain't it in *yet?*'"

———■———

An Irishman came to New York
And learned what the verb meant "to pork"
He moaned, "Oh, begorra
This ain't Gloccamorra
And sure as hell ain't County Cork!"

Outrageous

The cockney tart pulled back the sheet
And proved herself quite indiscreet
She said, "Listen, ducks,
Your lovemaking sucks
Besides, I'm turned off by webbed feet."

━■━

Last night in a sleazy motel
We fucked to a fine fare-thee-well
I begged, though, "Be gentle
And slightly less dental
My boobs don't wear teeth marks too well."

━■━

The children for hours had tried
When panting with eyes open wide
One said, "Guess we just squirm
'Til I fill you with sperm
—But how do I get it inside?"

Limericks

A clever slut tried to persuade
An IRS agent quite staid:
"I can't pay my tax
But if you'll relax
Perhaps we can work out a trade."

═ ■ ═

An act that we saw in the hills
Was good for some eyepopping thrills
This hot country bumpkin
For fucking a pumpkin
Was showered with ten-dollar bills.

═ ■ ═

The harlot's unfortunate stutter
Went thus as she laid a stonecutter:
"Although a good trick
I don't like your dick
Still, it's my b-bread and b-butter."

Outrageous

The saintly producer's rampage
Enveloped the actors in rage
"You should've made certain
They'd lowered the curtain
Before you did *that* on the stage!"

———■———

"Gee, warden, you're really a prince
And so understanding," said Vince
"When I got my pardon
It started to harden
And it's been that way ever since."

———■———

"The process of thinking I find
To be rather queer," I opined
"When I think of Kevin
The number eleven
Unbidden pops into my mind."

Limericks

Of course I believe you, Patrice
You're Martians, both you and your niece
—Or *am* I in trouble?
Am I seeing double
Or do you have four tits apiece?

———■———

"I'm gonna be late," cautioned Lynn
"But don't wait for me to begin
For fun while you're waiting
Just try masturbating
And when I arrive, I'll jump in."

———■———

Our guests have all gathered within
So I guess it's time to begin
And so, my dear bride
Let's both go inside
—But first wipe my cum off your chin."

Outrageous

The lass found adrift on the floes
Said, "If not for y'all I'd 'a froze"
Then, later that night
With no whale in sight
The first mate cried out, "Thar she blows!"

— ■ —

The suspect, beginning to cry,
Said, "I am that Most Wanted guy
I did make those messes
In sleeping girl's tresses
But I'm so ashamed I could die!"

— ■ —

Please, Doc, ain't this just "April Fool"?
I can't stand to look at you drool
Don't talk about waste
It's simply bad taste
To nibble like that on my stool.

Limericks

I gasped at the picture of Lynn
Whose rare, Mona Lisa-like grin
Was awfully pretty
But it was a pity
She wore nothing south of her chin.

= ■ =

The doctor's advice gave her cheer
As Granny redid her brassiere
"Routine masturbation
Improves circulation
—At *home*, Mrs. Lewis, not here!"

= ■ =

The laundry was finished at last
When Jean said, "I need it, and fast!"
So we just spread a sheet
And lay down in the street
Leaving passersby simply aghast.

Outrageous

After months in Manhattan poor Hope
Had come to the end of her rope
Allergic to liquor
She thought, "I'll die quicker
By washing down whiskey with dope."

An X-rated stud named Bernard
Did bit parts until he was starred
In porn films with class
Like "Dick Demitasse"
—This genre was dubbed "avant-hard."

The t.v. ad featured an elf
Who said from a pharmacist' shelf
"Attention late bloomers!
You've heard all the rumors
Now why not try Quick Dick yourself?"

Limericks

The good-humored tart made a quip
Concerning her favorite gyp:
"I met me this bloke
Who gave me a poke
And left me the clap for a tip!"

———■———

Some girls find it hard to let go
As did one who said to her beau
"Now, darling, I think
I can live with the stink
But these worms on your corpse have to go."

———■———

I thought to myself, "Go, Jerome!"
When I met this hooker in Rome
I wanted to spank her
But spotted a chancre
So I just shook hands and flew home.

Outrageous

Hi, honey, it's me, Uncle Roy
Let's both play that game we enjoy
Aw, someday you'll thank me
Now come here and spank me
And tell me I've been a bad boy.

———■———

The late Fuzzy Wuzzy the bear
Boo-hooed over having no hair:
"I'm king of the boobs
—I don't even have pubes!"
And then slashed both his wrists in despair.

———■———

A porno star famed for his dong
Was torn from his sleep by a throng
Who yelled, "Like the ruckus?
If you don't come fuck us
We'll stand here and scream all night long."

Limericks

"I'm shocked by your actions," said Bruce
"You don't seem the type to be loose"
She laughed, "Yes, I'm crass
But I wanted your ass
And that's why I'm called Mother *Goose.*"

═ ■ ═

The sex that we had was just grand
But please try to just understand
No, there's no other chick
Who's got claim on my dick
—I've fallen in love with my hand.

═ ■ ═

The savage, a muscular stud,
Said, "Here's how we ward off a flood:
My tribe for its voodoo
Combines hot, fresh doodoo
With semen and two cups of mud."

Outrageous

I'm sorry, I just have to speak
Because if it's pleasure you seek
You're at your own peril
To make it with Cheryl
'Cause she's had the syph for a week.

=■=

At first I was scared to presume
But he said he'd like to resume
It was great having sex
With my remarried ex
Each time his new wife left the room.

=■=

I'm sorry my health's out of whack
But go easy now on my crack
My love, you're courageous
—I'm highly contagious
Hey, where are you going? Come back!

Limericks

The vampire appeared with a bow
And fondly caressed my moist brow
He said, "Dear, your breath
Bears the perfume of death
So I'm really in love with you now."

—■—

The doctor was awfully nice
And on what he found quite precise:
"Please pull up your britches
The reason it itches
Ain't 'ants in your pants', son—it's lice!

—■—

We came to Osaka for tea
Where one bold teahouse employee
Though it was a no-no
Raised up her kimono
And showed how raw sushi can be.

Outrageous

Old Gramps was one hell of a chap
Who once as I woke from a nap
Was right there beside me
His dick deep inside me
And that's how I first got the clap.

———■———

Our scoutmaster showed a strange bent
Which made camping out an event
The very first night
He drank and got tight
And jerked off while sniffing our tent.

———■———

The bride left her groom in the lurch
And he, driven mad, took a perch
On top of the steeple
And pissed on those people
Who'd parked their cars nearest the church.

Limericks

No, that's not at all what I meant
I think you're one hell of a gent
I don't mean to taunt
It's just that I want
To give up cocksucking for Lent.

— ■ —

The minister said with a sigh,
"That Bob was one hell of a guy
So let us salute
Our friend who's en route
Now to that great twat in the sky."

— ■ —

The rajah's new wife sure was quick
To say, "Dear, I do hate to pick
But please have your eunuchs
Outfitted with tunics
Because all their scars make me sick."

67

Outrageous

Though some guys are glad to be gay
I'm here in the closet to stay
Though last night I beamed
And wept as I dreamed
That I'd been named "Queen for a Day."

———■———

The t.v. the store sent Eugene
Caused him to become quite obscene
For instead of a cord
It had clothes he deplored
And high heels instead of a screen.

———■———

I'm sorry, this thing must be ceased!
Your new lover's really a beast
Let me make one thing clear:
It's all right that you're queer
But, son, stick to humans at least!

Limericks

The guard said they'd changed all the plans
But this sounded grave to poor Hans
It *was* a beheading
—The rapist was shedding
The part that he thought with—his glans.

———■———

I really don't like to malign
But truth of it is you're a swine
To boot, you're a bastard
You shit-eating dastard
—But other than that, you're just fine.

———■———

Let's stop this before it's begun
I'm sorry, I don't think it's fun
Oh sure, sex if nifty
With men over fifty
But, Gramps, you're a hundred and one!

Outrageous

The question that I put to Paul
He answered like this in a drawl:
"You bet I love Lucy!
Her flesh is so juicy
That gravy ain't needed at all!"

— ■ —

I've been on the farm for so long
That, off it, I only do wrong
Last night, 'stead of sucking
I just started shucking
And, boy, what that did to Jim's dong!

— ■ —

"I like your new bath oil," said Pete
"Its fragrance is not oversweet
And, golly, your heiny
Tonight is so shiny
I'm watching myself as I eat."

Limericks

Indifference to school was widespread
'Til Miss Summerhays used her head
And gave kids incentive
To be more attentive
By shooting full moons as she read.

———■———

Please, love, I'm so totally beat
I can't even fondle your meat
I'll lay on my belly
And look at the telly
While you help yourself to a treat.

———■———

Although I'm the humblest of souls
It's true that I've reached all my goals
My cock's so gigantic
It spans the Atlantic
And I've made a fortune in tolls.

Outrageous

Hell no, I'm no damn ingenue
But still give this devil her due
Yes, it's quite true, Señor
That I'm only a whore
But I make more money than you.

—■—

A weightlifter worked on his pecs
Until they had grown so convex
The two were so heavy
They outweighed a Chevy
And he couldn't budge to have sex.

—■—

The peditrician McGrew
Enjoyed telling kids what to do
Whether children were shy
Or not he'd say, "I
Took off all my clothes—why don't you?"

Limericks

Her husband told Granny MacHeath
"I'm still a young man underneath
Though now we're in rockers
I still love your knockers
—I can? Wait, I'll take out my teeth."

—■—

The stud whom they nicknamed Big Ben
Was hung like a bull in a pen
But it was a shame
That each time he came
He took two days to harden again.

—■—

"The rape's left my whole life in shreds,"
I cried as we spoke to the Feds
"If Dr. Doolittle
Is granted acquittal
We sheep won't be safe in our beds."

Outrageous

The photos depict just a nun
So, looks like there's nought to be done
They're so unexplicit
They're barely illicit
Aw, hell! Vice Squad used to be fun.

—■—

The Johnsons, though often maligned
Remained always very refined
Each night little Malcolm
Was sent for the talcum
And dusted his mother's behind.

—■—

We sometimes do things no one should
And things that you'd think no one could
She gives me the strop
While I whimper, "Don't stop!
'Cause, baby, it just hurts so good!"

Limericks

The pervert was so inhumane
He had S & M on the brain
What he did to the owl
Was exceedingly foul
Though the owl felt no need to complain.

Although my good name's been maligned
I only reply, "Love is blind"
I know that it's odd
To be dating a cod
But haddocks are *so* hard to find.

Although this may sound like pure fiction
The Vatican's ordered eviction
Of twenty-three nuns
Who've tattooed their buns
With scenes of Our Lord's crucifixion.

Outrageous

A starfucking whore, no beginner
Was often invited to dinner
She had sex for free
With each nominee
And found that her twat knew the winner.

———■———

My sculpting career was quite through
I knew when I read the review:
"The artist has Venus
Equipped with a penis
While Zeus sets a record with two!"

———■———

Mis Idaho's speech was inventive
And kept all the judges attentive:
"I love baking bread
And give excellent head
Which I hope will give you incentive."

Limericks

His bedroom eyes cast such a spell
That lovers come running pell-mell
He's never caught short
Having girls in each port
—And guys in each airport as well!

—■—

We've fucked every night for a week
And now I'm afraid I must speak
To say please be gentle
For, though continental,
You happen, my dear, to be Greek!

—■—

Our story is Little Jack Horner
Who played with himself in the corner
He sat on his thumb
And moaned, "Here I come!"
And I wish I could make this one rhyme!

Outrageous

I sensed there was something amiss
Soon after we shared our first kiss
I said, "Listen, honey,
I don't think it's funny
'Cause if you're a girl, what is *this?*"

＝■＝

I wish I could be more genteel
But balling with you's an ordeal
Good God, it was murder!
Your cock's like a girder
It felt just like nine feet of steel.

＝■＝

Although she was free of disease
My conquest last night failed to please
I opened her legs
And drank to the dregs
But left with a mouthful of fleas.

Limericks

Though fearing the anger of God
The abbess uncovered her bod
And eased a dead fish up
The ass of the bishop
Who moaned, "I can tell—that's a cod!"

———■———

The doctor's report, although terse
Knocked out his most practical nurse:
"The late Mrs. Snyder
Had maggots inside her
And plenty to spare in her purse."

———■———

Her rank, indiscriminate drives
Cost innocent people their lives
When known how her habit
Had murdered a rabbit
Its kin stormed her cottage with knives.

Outrageous

I envy my married friend Joan
Whose husband's odd trait is well known
His left middle digit
Is big as a midget
And has a nice cock of its own.

＝■＝

The sly camel trader, Abou
Tried pimping in old Timbuktu
But some were confused
When Abou enthused
"Good evening, sir. One hump or two?"

＝■＝

My genie I kicked in the can
And yelled, "You're a real also-ran!
I didn't say "jackass"
I said I want black ass
—No donkey at *all*, fool—a man!"

Limericks

The bitch said, "Are you kidding—bitter?
The fact is, I've never felt fitter
Since they had me spayed
I'm free to get laid
'Cause I know I won't drop a litter."

———■———

Her actions erased any doubt
That she believes rules are to flout
In search of new tail
She straddled a whale
And spread her legs over the spout.

———■———

The strains of his sweet serenade
Advanced his attempts to persuade
Belinda to dally
Right there in the alley
Without any need to be paid.

Outrageous

Seduced by the scent of his musk
She sucked him from dawn until dusk
She loved this albino
Who called himself "Rhino"
Because of his singular "tusk."

Turned on by conspicuous sex
Jane put in a call to her ex
And later met Liam
Inside the museum
And brazenly nibbled his pecs.

The whore on one john was reliant
A wealthy man nicely compliant
To boot, Mr. Young
Was splendidly hung
—She called him her "Jolly Green Client."

Limericks

Our mobile bordello appeals
To many with lofty ideals
And since it's convenient
The clergy are lenient
With dear little "Pussy on Wheels."

———■———

Oppressed by a vague sense of dread
I stood at the foot of their bed
My folks were reluctant
To tell me what "fuck" meant
But offered to show me instead.

———■———

Our summer stock up at Lake Como
Was staged by an ex-major-domo
Who felt that the play
Had grown too cliché
You'll die when you see "Oklahomo!"

Outrageous

We both took a slug of the potion
And then greased our bodies with lotion
Though normally lazy
We just fucked like crazy
And so redefined "locomotion."

—■—

A sisterly chat at the spa
Went, "Sis, you take after our Ma
It looks like your clit's
As big as my tits
So, say, what cup size is its bra?"

—■—

In Venice a matchmaker's shop
Rang, *"Como se dice* 'to flop'?
Hey, what-a you mean-a
You don't like Regina
She's only 'ave crabs, you dump wop!"

Limericks

They all gasped when over liqeurs
Bob said as he eyed my contours
"Now listen up, kiddo,
I hear you're a widow
You want it? Bend over—it's yours."

— ■ —

Our young king had had too much scotch
And rudely insisted we watch
Once done with the peasants
He balled his pet pheasants
Once sure that we'd plucked every crotch.

— ■ —

No nightmare could ever devise
This guy whom we love to despise
Although it sounds scathing
He's not heard of bathing
—We call him the "Lord of the Flies."

Outrageous

One night while abroad with ol' Pinky
He said, "Damn, this hostel is dinky
I hear Finns are buxom
What say we go fuck some
And put the hell back in Helsinki."

———■———

Since some guys took longer to come
The tart felt a flat rate was dumb
So she bought a meter
And tricks could still eat her
But now they paid more for her bum.

———■———

With cum stains from forehead to chin
A hooker begged off Mr. Flynn:
"It's quarter to four
And my pussy is sore
'Cause last night the fleet floated in."

Limericks

A milkmaid once raped by the Huns
Said, "Now those were *men*" to some nuns
"Though truly the Viking
Is more to my liking
Because of his muscular buns."

—■—

We gasped when a migrant surveyor
Was booked as the wealthy purveyor
Of X-rated porn
Like "Barnyard At Morn"
Which starred seven goats and our mayor.

—■—

The sex clinic's head, Dr. Dickey
On t.v. said, "If you're a sickie
There's no obligation
Your first consultation
Will be on the house—it's a quickie."

Outrageous

She said to her twelve-year-old brat
"I think it's time we had a chat
Son, don't beat your meat
Out here in the street
That's Mommy's job, sweetheart—how's that?"

———■———

Your first wife, that is, Genevieve
Had chutzpah I couldn't believe
I'll never forget her
She puked on my sweater
Then wiped off her mouth on my sleeve.

———■———

You're some know-it-all, Angeline
Some expert! What are you—sixteen?
You've proved just how dumb
You are about cum
Of course it's supposed to be green!

Limericks

Her strange way of choosing a vet
Was something I'll never forget:
She played with their butts
And fondled their nuts
—The same way she'd chosen her pet.

Though offered sincerest regret
The customer bellowed at Chet
"What are you, a sickie?
I don't want a quickie
That's not what I meant by 'layette'!"

She struggled to keep her restraint
While telling Doc Jones her complaint:
"My poor little tits
Are no bigger than zits
—Why, the words 'acne cream' make me faint!"

Outrageous

Ground under the heel of inflation
Poor men look for cheap titillation
They find inner peace
And gain their release
Indulging in group masturbation.

— ■ —

A horny young egghead reflected
On thinkers whose work he'd inspected:
"I get so orgasmous
From reading Erasmus
The coeds must all be protected."

— ■ —

We stock at our video store
The world's first mechanical whore
You just place a coin
Way up in her groin
And then, like with pinball, you score.

Limericks

In Storybookland things were hopping
Skirts lifted while leggins were dropping
Why, old Mother Hubbard
Got laid in the cupboard
And came for an hour without stopping.

———■———

Hold on now, I'll open my coat
No wonder they callo you "Deep Throat"!
But let's be discreet
So, darling, don't bleat
Or your father will hear, the old goat!

———■———

Do take my advice and steer clear
Of Mary's buffet over here
I noticed a booger
Adrift in the sugar
What's that in your coffee—oh, *dear!*

Outrageous

"I'm so steeped in whoredom," wailed Bree,
"I doubt that I'll every break free!
"Cause I'm just such a mess
Once, when toasted, 'Success!'
I answered, 'Okay. Which is he?' "

— ■ —

She feared that he wouldn't believe her
But nonetheless said Mrs. Cleaver:
"That boy Eddie Haskell
Is really a rascal
Ward, look what he did to the Beaver!"

— ■ —

As Grampa's days dwindled he clung
To memories he'd made while still young
Of lifting girls' bustles
To nibble their muscles
And then picking pubes from his tongue.

Limericks

I felt my complexion go white
At hearing these words from Doc White:
"Relax, those aren't scabs
They're nothing but crabs
So big, though, we're in for a fight."

— ■ —

She loved when in bed he would flex
His quite unsurpassable pecs
His major in college
Had been carnal knowledge
—He had a B.A. in Group Sex.

— ■ —

Our tennis match ended when Ed
Exposed what distressed him in bed
I said, "This is *short?*
It's the length of the court!
Of course, it *is* thinner than thread."

Outrageous

The story of Friar Marcel
Is truly a sad one to tell
The elderly monk
Awoke to a skunk
Asleep on his face. It was hell!

——■——

They say that a past Prince of Wales
Said this to a couple of Gaels:
My friends, that felt good
I knew that it would
But please next time do trim your nails."

——■——

When her favorite film star came in
The waitress proposed with a grin:
You can have all my tips
Let me just put my lips
Halfway from your knees to your chin.

Limericks

The newlyweds asked that a broom
And butter be sent to their room
We eavesdropped outside
And soon heard the bride
Begin to sing "Here Comes the Groom."

—■—

The Martian invasion I swear
Gave everyone here quite a scare
It was anyone's guess
What they did to poor Bess
That made her give birth to a chair.

—■—

The bride, looking pale as a wraith,
Said, "Love just how strong is your faith
I've been saving the worst
You're not quite my first
In fact you're the hundred and eighth."